Dogs We Love

Text by Alfred Barbou followed by a
"Portrait of the Dog" by Buffon

Translated by Blanche Michaels

A Pierre Waleffe Book

Minerva

"...A synod was held in which the question of whether or not animals had a soul was discussed very seriously: would good dogs go to paradise and bad ones, who stole slices of leg of lamb, burn in hell eternally. The denial of the soul was voted: it is enough for the honor of the species that the question was posed.

The dog has been esteemed and loved by all the peoples on earth and he has deserved this affection for he renders services that have made him man's best friend.

If we are to study a species so intimately involved with our own, which has shared our life since time immemorial and never stopped being useful, we must start by mentioning the historic legends to which its existence has given rise.

People never tire of trying to explain the cosmogonic myths and legends of the different peoples of ancient times; it is no less interesting to recall the great role played by dogs in the very distant past.

The veneration of fear they inspired, the superstitions of which they have been the object, the honors given them prove that they occupied an important place in societies no longer in existence today.

There is no nation which has not paid attention to these quadrupeds or given them a special role in its history.

Of all animals the dog is unquestionably the one most frequently mentioned by the authors of bygone times.

According to a 19th century author the dog was known to Adam's sons; as a matter of fact, Abraham's faithful servant related that Abel's body, abandoned by Cain to the mercy of wild beasts, was

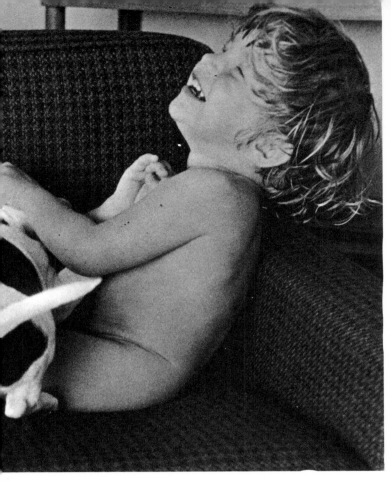

From time immemorial, the child and the dog have understood each other. The dog's love of children is evident on all occasions.

defended by the dog that guarded his flocks.

The Books of Tobit and Deuteronomy mention dogs often. The dog in Tobit is well-known for he made a long trip to announce to Tobia's blind father the impending arrival of his son and the end of his misfortunes. Already at that time the dog had become the symbol of devotion.

The dog is revered and adored by the Egyptians because he warns man and is looked upon as a friend.

A great number of embalmed dogs have been taken out of the tombs of ancient Egypt. These animals were mourned and buried with great ceremony; they gave birth to a deity.

Anubis was an Egyptian god worshipped in the form of a dog or a man with a dog's head.

If one is to believe Plutarch, Anubis was the son of Osiris and Nephthys, his sister, who was married to the god Eyphon. Isis, having discovered that Osiris had drawn near to Nephtys in error, looked for the child born of this adultery, whom Nephtys, afraid of her husband, had abandoned; she found him with the help of her dogs and took care of him through childhood.

Later on, when Isis went in search of the body of Osiris, who had been assassinated

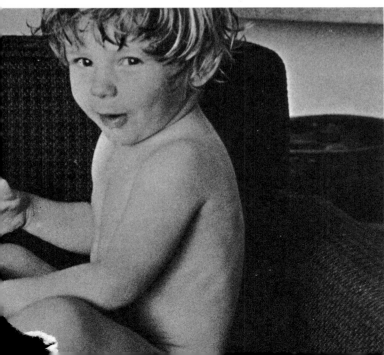

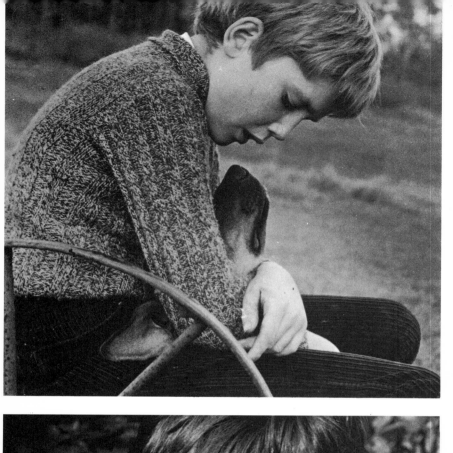

Confidence and Affection.

A fine guard of Great Danes!

by Typhon, her faithful companion was Anubis, who had put on the skin of a dog. Anubis was worshipped along with Osiris and Isis, since he was considered to be the vigilant and inseparable guardian of these two deities. In one of the administrative departments of Middle Egypt, whose capital the Greeks had named *Cynopolis* (city of dogs), he received special honors; the dog, dedicated to him as a living symbol, was fed at the treasury's expense. Moreover, worship of the dog extended to all parts of Egypt. Juvenal wrote: *oppida tota canem venerantur* (the dog is worshipped in every town). And Herodotus noted that when a dog died all those living in the house shaved their heads as a sign of mourning, then buried the corpse in a consecrated box.

Because he was confused with the animal representing him, Anubis was the butt of jokes by the satirist Lucian. In one of his dialogues, Lucian portrays Momus as trying to turn this "barking dog" out of the Council of Gods. Barking dog, labrator, is the epithet given to Anubis by all the Latin poets. Propertius was indignant with Cleopatra for daring to place her barking Anubis on as high a level as Jupiter.

These jokes did not stop the cult of Anubis from passing to Greece first of all and then to Rome, where it was maintain-

From the concierge to society women: every-body's friend.

ed for a long time, even alongside the Christian religion.

Several authors, among them Plutarch and Lucan, made Anubis the symbol of the horizon separating the upper from the lower world. Anubis uncovers the sun at sunrise, brings it to our hemisphere, hides it from sight by sending it back through the western door to the lower hemisphere and then takes up the moon, whose course he likewise follows.

The dog was Anubis's symbol because it can discern objects at night as well as in daytime and is man's faithful friend just as Anubis was the faithful companion of the Sun and the Moon.

The god Anubis was usually represented with the body of a man and the head of a dog. A statue in black granite at the villa Albani is quite remarkable: the head, combining the features of cat, lion and dog, is crowned by a kind of miter covered in folds falling onto the shoulders. Behind this headdress, called *claft* by Egyptologists, there is a disk representing the sun, the moon or perhaps a kind of halo.

Sometimes Anubis is portrayed wholly as a dog, in which case he has a pointed snout and the greyhound's svelte body with pricked up ears and a hanging, very bushy tail.

From time immemorial, the dogs perso-

13

nified by Anubis have inspired a superstitious dread in the inhabitants of the Nile Valley, who consider the barking they hear during the night to be of ill omen. If in the Hebrew books, in the Book of Leviticus in the Old Testament, the dog is not on the threefold list of clean and unclean animals, it is undoubtedly because the first lawgivers of the 12 tribes had learned to revere and fear the dog while they were living in the country of Anubis.

Getting back to the worship inspired by the dog in ancient times, we should remember that the holy books of India and Persia confirm it.

In Sanskrit the dog is known by more than 50 names, which amply proves that already in ancient times there was a great variety of dogs. The name which recurs the most often is *çvan,* a word which, according to the etymologists, has given rise to all the names by which the dog is known in the languages of Europe. In the *Zend-Avesta,* the sacred book of the Parsees and monument of Aryan civilization, the dog is often mentioned. It is considered as one of the three animals that the Zoroastrian religion commands its faithful to feed: "When a dog is six months old," says one passage in the book, "a young girl should feed it; this girl will have the same merit as if she had

A silent exchange
but how heartfelt.

Alone, absolutely alone of all the animals, dogs have made or inspired these gestures.

protected fire, son of Ormuzd."

In ancient Egypt dogs were fed regularly, being given the produce of a specific area of land and Diodorus of Sicily noted that during the famines which laid the country waste, the inhabitants were driven to devouring each other rather than touch a dog.

When the Egyptians had sores or wounds, they had those animals lick them which they held in high regard, saying that their saliva was preferable to the most precious ointments. When a dog died in the house, the inhabitants went into mourning; anyone who killed a dog was killed in turn and anyone who mistreated a dog was severely punished.

Dogs were not only raised to the rank of deity but some were made kings.

Speaking of Norway, a traveler recalled that in a small valley in the Uplands he had seen a memorial dedicated to a dog. He then told the following story that he had heard from the peasants: "King Eystein had been expelled from his country by his subjects. He returned with a large army, crushed the rebels and, to punish them for the offense committed against him, condemned them to recognize as their legitimate sovereign either a slave or a dog; the poor people preferred a dog. They were given one called Saur, who

On the right: A woman officer in the U.S. Air Force prepares the message to be carried by Bumble, waiting attentively at her side. He is a mixture of Beagle and Pointer, eight years old.

took the title Majesty as soon as he mounted the throne. The new king had a court, officers, men at arms, a house and sycophants.

A philospher, using the laws of metempsychosis, proved that a great man's soul had passed into the body of this large watchdog. A grammarian showed that this noble animal could pronounce two words of the Norwegian language distinctly and could bark a third word.

Whenever he appeared before his people, he was escorted by a large guard and if the weather was bad, liveried servants carried him in their arms so that his paws should not get wet. This dog ruled for almost three years.

He issued several edicts, sealing them and his judgments with the tip of his nail. Just when the inhabitants of the region were becoming accustomed to this curious king and beginning to recognize his good qualities, he died, victim of his devotion and heroism.

One day he was sitting on grazing ground near one of the flocks of sheep which he had formerly guarded and that he always enjoyed seeing again.

All of a sudden a raging wolf came out of the forest and sprang at a lamb. The king wanted to run to help the innocent victim. Instead of curbing his courageous

ardor, treacherous counsellors urged him on to face the danger. He rose, betook himself to the scene of the struggle and was torn to death by his adversary's merciless teeth. He was given a magnificent funeral and buried near a hill which still bears the name Hill of Sorrow."

Aelianus, the Greek writer, referred to some of the peoples of Ethiopia who, out of respect, chose a dog as their sovereign and Pliny related that the Toembars did the same. This small tribe consulted their ruler before embarking on any undertaking: they interpreted the dog's behavior and gestures and made their plans accordingly. Undoubtedly a custom fit for barbarous peoples but how many nations have been less well-inspired by confiding their destinies to a man!

Sacred dogs were known in many places but those of which Aelianus speaks are the most famous. "On Mount Etna in Sicily stands a temple of Vulcan which has walls, sacred woods and a fire that burns eternally. There are also sacred dogs around the temple and the woods. As if they were creatures of reason, these animals caress with their tails those who approach the temple and the woods devoutly. On the other hand, they bite and tear at those whose hands are unclean and chase away men and women who come only for a

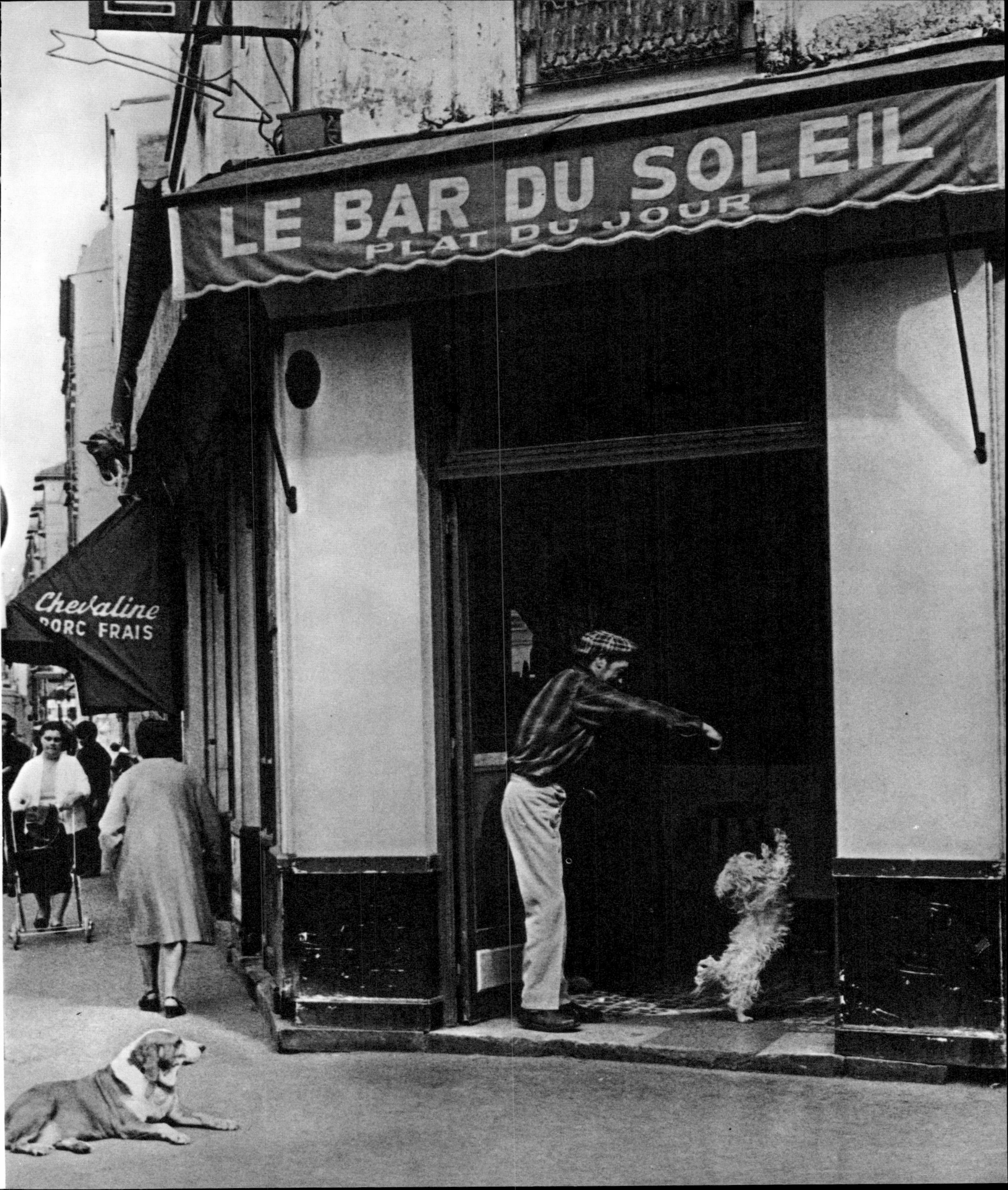
LE BAR DU SOLEIL
PLAT DU JOUR
Chevaline
PORC FRAIS

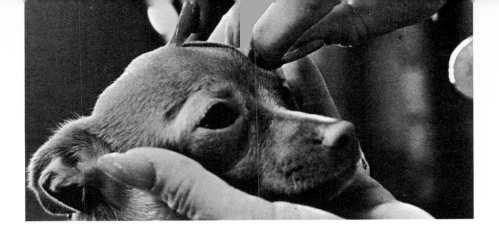

rendez-vous."

"On the island of Ceylon, the king has no title, but out of respect for him his subjects divest themselves of their human quality while speaking to him. If the prince asks someone where he comes from, the answer is: "*Your dog* comes from such and such a place." If he wants to know how many children one has, the answer, in reference to one's wife and children, should be: "My bitch has given your dog two children."

North American Indians bestowed an exalted origin on the dog. "After having created the sky, the earth and the animals, the Great Spirit wanted to do better by creating man and woman. As he held in his powerful hand the matter to be used for this creation, he divided it into two equal parts and breathed life into the first part which was man. But since he wanted man to be master of everything, he cut off a piece from the matter he was going to use to create woman, and with it he made the dog which he placed at the couple's feet."

If we go from the legends of India, Persia, Egypt and America and pass to the stories of Mythology, we find equally interesting information.

Cerberus, with his three mouths, was the most renowned of all dogs. In former times, everything went by threes: Isis, Osiris and Horus; Jupiter, Neptune and Pluto, the three brother gods of the Greek world; the three Fates, the three Furies, Alecto, Tisiphone and Megaera; the three judges of Hades; the three mouths of Cerberus.

However, this incorruptible gatekeeper of Hades was also called the beast with one hundred heads because of the snakes that bristled around his neck. Hesiodus said he had 50 heads; Horace thought there were 100 but in the ancient monuments Cerberus is shown with three heads, a respectable number, and that is the way he is described by almost all the poets, including Virgil who portrayed him in the sixth book of the *Aeneid.*

According to mythology, it was the task of this ferocious four-legged, three-mouthed guardian to prevent the souls, condemned to eternal tortures, from leaving Hades, Pluto's empire. An obol, a tiny coin, and a cake were placed in the tombs of those who died at that time, the obol to pay the passage in Charon's ferry, the cake to soften Cerberus's ferocity.

Who was this terrifiyng guardian? Quintus Calaber of Smyrna has told of Cerberus's birth in the following way: "Typhon, the giant, having found Echidna in a cave at the doors of hell, close to

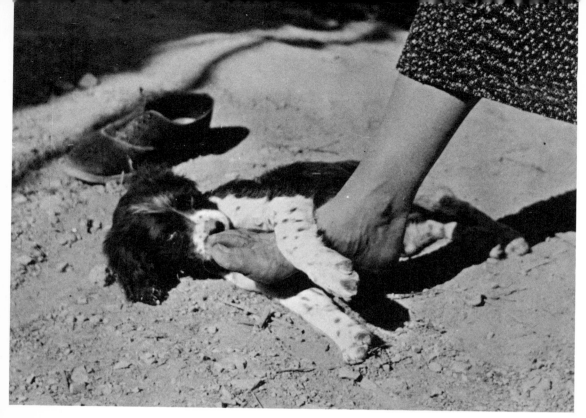

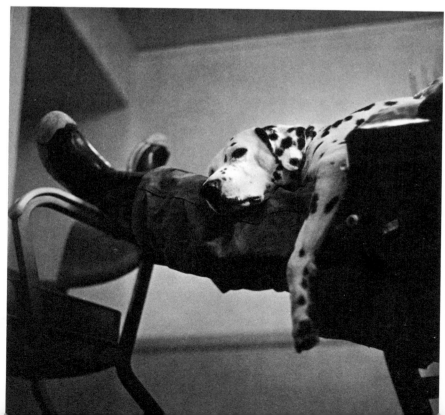

Many pictures in this book are eloquent enough not to need captions, for these would only take away from their meaning.

the abode of night, raped her: the fruit of this passion was Cerberus, who always remained attached to the somber shores, guarding the Plutonian empire."

Nonetheless, it seems that Cerberus left the underworld once in the following circumstances: Hercules, who in a fit of madness had killed his children, was ordered to live at Tiryns, to serve Eurystheus for twelve years and to perform twelve great "labors" which he accomplished thanks to his strength and bravery. Eurystheus ordered Hercules to bring Cerberus up from the lower world. Hercules, condemned to obedience and trusting to his courage, did not hesitate to try his luck. He went down to the shores of the Styx after having passed through a cave situated near the promontory of Taenarum. From there he descended into the underworld and delivered Theseus, who had come with Pirithoüs to carry off Persephone but had been seized by Pluto and chained to a rock.

In order to succeed, Hercules had to battle with all his might since Pluto had given him permission to carry Cerberus to the upper world, provided he did so without force of arms. Cerberus put up a terrible resistance but Hercules managed in the end to attach the dog with diamond chains and carried him away. Seeing the light of day, the horrible four-legged monster exuded a livid black foam from his blood-stained mouth. According to the fable, as the liquid fell onto the rock it turned to aconite, a terrible poison which has become a valuable remedy, thanks to modern science.

While being dragged along by Hercules, Cerberus let out such dreadful howls that a traveler, meeting them on the way, died of fright.

Eurystheus, satisfied with the way Hercules had carried out this task, freed Cerberus who joyously returned to his place at the door to the underworld from whence he has never since budged.

In the Middle Ages, Cerberus became a demon—there are monuments to prove it! He had a very distinguished place in demonology, being accorded the rank of marquis. Nineteen legions obeyed his commands and, strange as it may seem, his job was to teach fine arts and oratory to those who summoned him to help them. Here we have a patron whom artists and lawyers no longer seek out but who was formerly looked to for protection and consulted from three o'clock in the afternoon to the close of day.

At the end of the 17th century, a council passed judgment on the witch, Marie Martin, who was convicted of having been

"More docile than man, the dog adapts himself to the gestures, the manners and all the habits of those who give him orders: he takes on the tone of the house where he lives." (Buffon)

present at a meeting presided over by Cerberus the demon. The unfortunate woman was condemned to be hanged and strangled; she appealed in vain to the parliament of Paris which rejected her petition for mercy and she was executed on July 25, 1686.

Cerberus was held in dread as a devil until the 18th century, this was a survival of the Greeks' mythological legend; but he also has an obvious relationship to the Indian dogs of Yama one of which was called *Cerbura* or *Karbura*, meaning spotted. Consequently, the Greeks' imagination had taken possession of a tradition from a primitive epoch. The Hindus believed in the existence of two dogs of the underworld; they laid out their dead on the skin of a cow or a goat that had been sacrificed close to the funeral pyre and in the hands they placed the animal's kidneys, a dainty morsel destined to appease the dogs of the god of death.

When there were no animals to sacrifice, rice balls replaced the kidneys. This custom was at the origin of the Greeks' belief in the honey cake.

The Scandinavians shared the same superstition: for them a dog called *Garmr* was the guardian of the underworld. This monstrous dog whose chest was stained with blood, howled unceasingly and was chained to the entrance of the underworld. But there is a touching side to this superstition, for if the dead person had given bread to the poor during his lifetime, he always found, when in the underworld, a way to calm the guardian's ferocity.

The Swedes believed in the existence of a dog who was keeper of the infernal. regions, with power to protect the dead against evil spirits.

The dog who guides souls was still found in the popular superstitions of 19th century America. Some old tales of that country relate that the souls of the dead went to the parish priest of Brastar whose dog then accompagnies them as they go to embark on their journey across the seas. The creaking of the wheels of the *chariot of the dead,* laden with souls, is then heard in the air.

When a son was born, the Romans sacrificed dogs to the goddess Mona-Geneta. They believed that in this way they could successfully protect their children. There is evidence that worship of this kind was very general. The Sicilians for instance kept 1,000 dogs in their god's temples.

In his writings, Pliny mentions the names of several peoples whose kings always had a dog by their side to inspire vigilance and kindness in them. These

animals were allowed into the Athenians' palaces where they were present at the most sumptuous banquets and the most solemn ceremonies and they had their place at occasions of public rejoicing.

The Athenians sacrificed dogs to Hecate and had the idea that if they were licked by these animals they became pure.

There are numerous stories about dogs among the Greeks; some touching ones show very well the tenderness felt towards dogs by the nation once renowned as the most polite and the most civilized. When Ulysses returned to Ithaca after an absence of 20 years, nobody recognized him in his beggar's rags. The sorrowful hero was walking pensively with Eumaeus, the shepherd, when an old dog came up to him, wagged its tail and ears as a sign of joy and licked his hands. It was Ulysses' dog, immortalized by Homer in the 17th book of the *Odyssey.* Eumaeus said to Ulysses, who had been moved to tears by the animal's long fidelity: "This is Argus, who belonged to a hero who died in a faraway land. Ah! if only he still had the courage and the kindness he had when Ulysses left for the Trojan fields! Now he pines away on the dunghill; since Ulysses' death far from his country, the lazy, indifferent women of this palace no longer take care of his dog." After licking his

It is well known that when his master is away, the dog is happy and proud to keep something that belongs to him or to watch over his things.

master's hand, Argus died.

In Greece, dogs were also involved in politics, as the following story shows. We do not guarantee its authenticity in any way but, since it comes from Alexandre Dumas, let him tell it in his own words.

"There is no one who has not noticed the way in which dogs approach each other or who has not tried to understand their manner of "shaking hands". Some naturalists think that they have solved the problem, but I prefer the Ancients' legend to the explanation given by the Moderns.

Pliny claims that the dogs of Laconia wanted to set themselves up in a republic after witnessing the defeat of Hippias and the triumph of Clisthenes' laws, events that introduced the era of democracy in Greece. But in order that their canine republic should not be subject to the upheavals through which their ancestors had lived during the different experiments already made, the dogs decided to make sure of Jupiter's aid by demanding his permission and, as it were, his protection.

Consequently, on a parchment they drew up a petition to the god of thunder and gave it to a greyhound to carry to Mount Olympus. To honor the messenger, who was leaving with the petition between his teeth, 50 of the most eminent dogs were chosen to accompany him to the

"The dog, faithful to man, will always conserve a degree of superiority over the other animals." (Buffon)

"It can be said that the dog is the only animal whose fidelity is put to the test: the only one who invariably knows his master and the friends of the house; the only one who realizes when a stranger arrives; who hears his name and recognizes the voices of 'his' family."

"The worship of the dog in ancient times is confirmed in the holy books of India and Persia: "When a dog is six months old," says a passage in the Zend-Avesta, "a young girl should feed it: this girl will have the same merit as if she had protected fire, son of Ormuzd.""

Accustomed to waiting, his attention is always on the qui-vive.

...Always drawn towards man.

Most dogs are voracious, gourmands, sometimes gourmets: a natural tendency and perhaps also a form of epicurism.

River Eurotas...Upon reaching it they saw that, due to a terrible storm which had risen the night before, the river, ordinarilly shallow enough to be forded, was close to overflowing its banks.

This did not dismay the messenger since he swam like an otter but he thought that something might happen to the petition during the crossing. Where was it to be put so that the water would not obliterate the letters? One of the escorting dogs who was considered to be the son of a fox because of his shrewdness and wiles, cried out like Archimedes:

—Eureka! that is to say, I've got it!

He then took the petition from between the greyhound's teeth, rolled it like a cigarette and stuffed it...where we were taught that prisoners hid the files they made with watch springs. Reassured as to the message's fate, the greyhound jumped bravely into the water, crossed the Eurotas without mishap and when he reached the other shore, bade farewell to his companion with a wave of his paw. Then, bounding forward at full speed in the direction of Mount Olympus, he disappeared. He has never been seen since.

This long and disturbing absence explains the manner in which dogs have approached each other since then, for in each unknown dog they hope to find the messenger

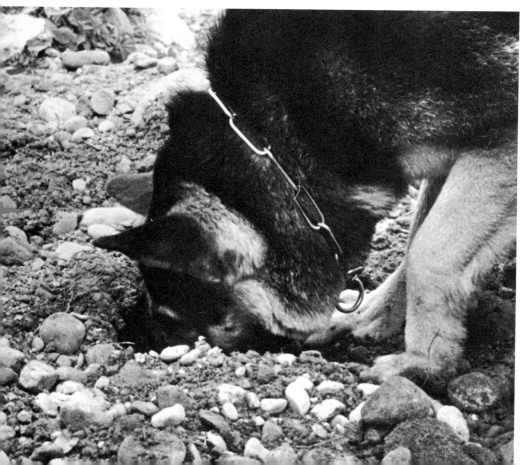

"To imagine for a moment that the canine species had never existed is to make ourselves aware of its importance in nature's order." (Buffon).

bringing them Jupiter's answer.

Now, some authors, who have done their best to discover what might have become of the unfortunate ambassador claim that he obtained Jupiter's authorization, but having been surprised by a thick fog as he was coming down from Olympus, he got lost, walked straight across the Ocean on polar ice and arrived in America. There he became the Washington of the dogs of the Prairies who, as everyone knows, have lived in a republic in the middle of the New World for the last 2,000 years."

This charming legend has been rejuvenated and been transferred from paganism to the Christian religion. The following is the modern version: At the end of the Thirty Years' War, some dogs came together in a German field to tell each other their troubles. During the meeting, the speakers pointed out that men, dogs' debtors, gave them only bones to gnaw and beat them. After a vote taken by rising or remaining seated, the assembly decided to send a delegate to complain to the Pope.

The Pope received the messenger kindly, listened sympathetically and acceded to his request, giving him a bull in which man's duties to dogs were set forth clearly. The delighted messenger set out for home

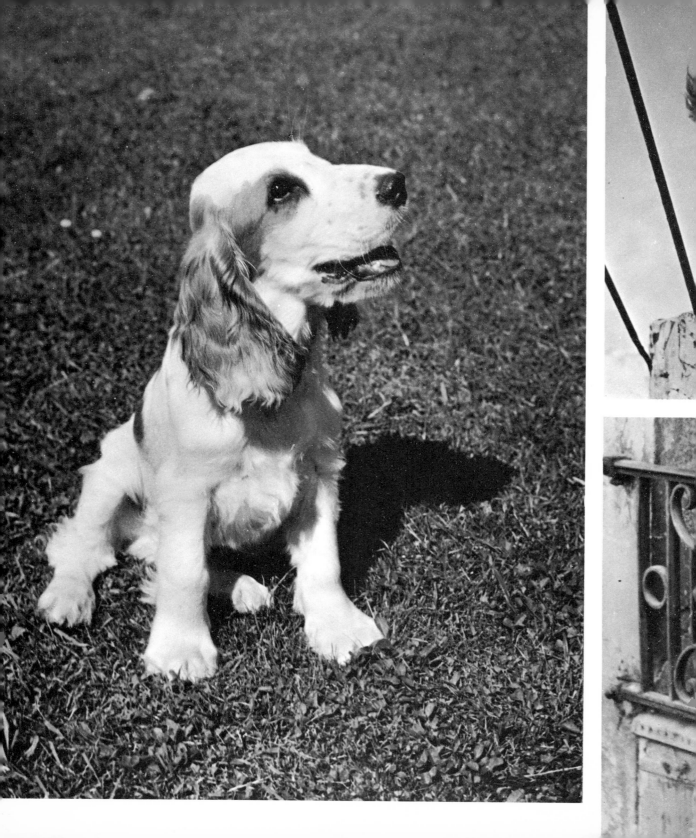

The dog always be-
haves a little as if
he were on a hunt.

Inclining his head, to understand better: no friend of dogs is insensitive to such expressions.

holding the bull in his mouth. Reaching the shores of the Rhine and finding no bridge nearby, the dog jumped into the water but it was so pure, so limpid at that spot that he saw his own image and joyfully started to bark; the Papal bull was carried away by the current; the dog was drowned trying to retrieve it and neither he nor the bull was ever seen again.

In desperation, the dogs sent the Pope a second messenger who, as well received as the first, was given a new bull. He managed to bring it back to the conclave using the same method that had been employed by the Greek dog.

Great was the joy of his friends who immediately wondered where to put the precious parchment to ensure its safety. A cat, who had been admitted to their company, proposed that it be hidden at the top of a neighboring tower; this plan was accepted but some time later, as men's ways hadn't changed at all, the dogs wanted to have the bull again and use it. Alas, when the cat reached the spot where he had hidden the parchment, only its remains were to be seen: rats had eaten the bull. Ever since then, continues the legend, dogs have hated cats and cats rats.

We must not forget to mention Saint

The animal, at the bottom right, makes us think of Diogenes; but philosophical as the dog may be, he is, alas, not gifted with the resources of a great mind and does not appreciate living in a barrel.

Roch's dog which Rubens painted. According to the legend, every day the hero's faithful companion carried to his master in the desert a loaf, received from an unknown hand. In a poem Victor Hugo, who loved dogs and likened himself to the saint, recalled the walks he used to take with his poodle in the village of Chelles:

"When I arrive with my poodle
The devout and comely town of Chelles
Believes that it is seeing
St. Roch and his dog St. Roquet
Escaping from their seclusion."

In the Christian religion, the dog has played quite a modest role; however, a synod was held in which the question of whether or not animals had a soul was discussed very seriously. Would good dogs, respectful of property, go to paradise and bad ones, who stole slices of leg of lamb, burn in hell eternally. It was decided that dogs have no soul but it is enough for the honor of the species that the question was posed.

Original sin was also not accepted although the philosopher Malebranche suggested ironically that perhaps dogs had eaten the forbidden bone. From time immemorial, the dog has been considered to be better than man. In St. Luke's Gospel we read: "And a man called Lazarus was begging, lying at his door and covered with sores; he was hoping to be able to eat his fill from the crumbs that fell from the table of the rich but no one gave him anything; only the dogs came and licked his sores."

Thus does tradition represent the dog as always having been so good that he comes to the aid of men abandoned by their fellows. This fact alone should suffice to make us cherish these animals who are faithful into death and whom neither sickness nor poverty can put to flight.

The most noble and courageous acts redound to the honor of the canine race. Naturallly endowed with courage, and thanks to man's training, the dog has acquired a total disregard for his own safety, to the point of heroism.

We have been able to inspire in these companions, our four-legged friends, all our passions from the noblest to the basest. The whole scale of human behavior is represented in the species, from the valiant knights to the industrial barons.

The Greeks often used dogs to guard their military camps and forts; among others, the citadel of Corinth had a garrison of mastiffs, the most beautiful breed of dogs in ancient times. That type of

Faithful to the laws of nature.

mastiff is now extinct but it is claimed that two admirable marble statues in the Vatican give an exact likeness of it.

All that is left of this proud race now seems to be the watchdog or the shepherd dog descended from the dogs of *Laconia.*

Among the famous dogs of antiquity, let us pick out Xanthippus's which, during the battle of Salamis, ran into the sea barking at the enemy, and the valiant dog which, fighting at Marathon with the Greeks against the Persians, was covered with wounds. He was honored as a hero.

Plutarch stated quite definitely that there was no canine garrison in the citadel of Athens; but there certainly was one in the stronghold of Corinth, which was guarded on the outside by an advance post of 50 dogs placed as sentries on the seashore. One night when the soldiers were drunk, the enemy landed; the 50 dogs fought like lions and 49 of them were killed on the spot. The last one, called Soter, ran to the city and gave the alarm, waking the soldiers who repulsed the enemy.

The Senate decreed that Soter should wear a silver collar with the inscription: "Soter, protector and savior of Corinth". In honor of the other dogs, a marble monument was built on which their names, along with Soter's were inscribed.

The name Soter means savior in Greek and in mythology was a surname given to Jupiter, Bacchus and Apollo. Later this same name was applied to several Egyptian and Syrian kings and in Christian martyrology there is a Pope called Soter.

An advance post of dogs was likewise charged with guarding the Capitol in Rome and these vigilant sentinels carried out their mission with all the zeal expected of them. However, there was one occasion when they were found wanting.

When the Gauls, led by Brennus, besieged Rome, all the Romans capable of carrying arms shut themselves up in the Capitol while the old men, who had made up their minds to die, remained in the abandoned city.

Having captured the city, the Gauls then tried one night to scale the walls of the fortress and, hoisting each other up, climbed the escarpments without making enough noise to wake the dogs, who had dropped off to sleep, weakened by hunger. Howewer, when the attackers reached the doors, the dogs opened their eyes and were about to start barking. The Gauls closed the dogs' mouths in the same way as that of Cerberus had been closed, by throwing pieces of bread to them, which they devoured.

Luckily for the Romans, Juno's sacred

geese proved less manageable, and they cried out thus giving the alarm. The garrison came immediately and hurled the enemy down to the bottom of the rocks.

Ever since, when the anniversary of this deliverance was celebrated in Rome, a goose, for whom the laurels of triumph were reserved, was led about on a chariot. A dog tied to the chariot brought up the rear.

It would be tedious to recall everything that was attributed to dogs in ancient times, so we shall content ourselves with the major deeds which clearly prove that in former times dogs were useful auxiliaries in time of war, proud fighters who never deserted their posts and knew how to die. There are a thousand proofs of this in the pages of history. Strabo relates that the Gauls used dogs in war as if they were foreign soldiers. Appian writes that the

early kings of Gaul "had for their permanent bodyguard a corps of dogs who were bold and valiant in combat and never abandoned their masters."

They fought at their masters' side and Pliny recalls that, when the Cimbri had been defeated by Marius, the Romans had to begin the battle again with their dogs.

The knights of Rhodes used these good companions for the advance posts, and for patrols and they did so frequently. An antique, bronze statue found at Herculaneum, and placed in the museum in Naples, depicts dogs wearing breastplates, who are defending a citadel attacked by fully armed soldiers.

Herodotus writes that Cyrus gathered together a great number of large watchdogs for the war. He then assigned them to four cities, whose inhabitants had to feed them. The Celts had regiments of dogs

...according to their master's social milieu.

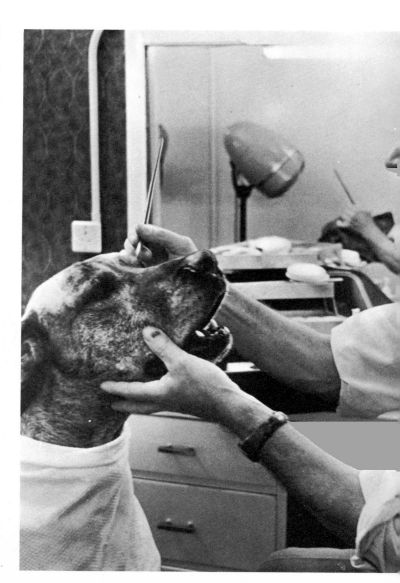

How many masters would have wanted to be ill in place of their dogs. At any rate, there are excellent ways of taking good care of the latter.

with collars studded with steel spikes and covered with breastplates.

Pliny relates that the Colophonians and the Castabalians owned cohorts of dogs, prepared for war, which fought in the front lines without ever giving up. Valuable, most reliable and most faithful allies, who did not cost a penny in pay.

Massinissa, who had little faith in men, used dogs as guards.

Many peoples have trained dogs to wipe out ambushes. Another of Pliny's stories concerns the king of the Garamantes, who was driven from his throne and managed to get it back only with the help of a company of 200 dogs. Pliny was a great admirer of these useful auxiliaries who, said he, once joined in battle never gave up, never ran away from the enemy and were not at all demanding as far as honors, advancement and pay were concerned.

Later on, dogs were used against cavalry; the dogs wore a breastplate to the front of which was attached a scythe and a vessel full of fire. The horses, tormented by the burns and the dogs' bites, ran away. In the Middle Ages this was called the war of the dogs against the cavalry.

The use of war dogs continued during the Middle Ages. The history of England is full of stories of great battles in which

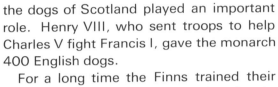

the dogs of Scotland played an important role. Henry VIII, who sent troops to help Charles V fight Francis I, gave the monarch 400 English dogs.

For a long time the Finns trained their dogs to hunt men. Elsewhere, they fought against the enemy's dogs. At Grandson, the mountain dogs of the Swiss confederates, began the action against the dogs of Burgundy.

The Spaniards used dogs in America. All by themselves, the dogs of Vasco Nunez strangled more than 2,000 Indians. Half the credit for the Spaniards' conquests in Mexico and Peru must go to dogs; they were trained to hunt the Indians as our dogs hunt deer or hare and they were allowed to tear to pieces the Indians they found. It is said that Peruvian dogs long to avenge themselves against the Spaniards.

History has preserved the name of the famous dog *Bérésillo,* who was responsible for as much slaughter as 100 Castilian highwaymen and received high pay, double rations and military rank.

At the battle of Caxamalca, the dogs in Pizarro's army behaved so valiantly that the Spanish court, grateful for their heroic deed, decreed that the dogs would be paid regularly, like the other troops.

During the campaigns of 1769 and

1774, the Turks and above all the Bosnians took along with them a large number of dogs who watched over the camp's security and tore to bits the enemies who ventured too close.

In 1788, at the siege of Dubicza, the Turkish dogs attached to the front line troops defended themselves victoriously against the Austrian patrols.

The French dogs of Santo Domingo also have their history.

Everywhere, no matter what kind of service he is asked to render, the dog understands and with unequalled self-sacrifice and matchless courage, he carries out his master's command.

Man's cruelty has turned good and devoted animals into savage beasts who eat men. One is reminded of the appalling and often-quoted remark by a Haitian Spaniard to a fellow scoundrel: "Lend me a quarter of an Indian for my watchdogs' lunch; I'll return it tomorrow or the day after."

The story of the poodle *Moffino* is still told in Milan. During the 1812 expedition to Russia he followed his master, a soldier in Prince Eugene Beauharnais' army. During the rout of Napoleon's troops, the two companions were separated at the crossing of the Berezina river and the Milanese soldier returned home alone.

One year after the soldier's return, a poor, emaciated animal, all skin and bone, turned up on the soldier's doorstep. When the people in the house tried to chase the dog away, he howled pitifully. He was such a horrible skeleton of a dog that the soldier himself was ready to chase him away with a kick when, suddenly, looking at the animal more closely, he bent down and called Moffino. Hearing this name, the poor creature barked with joy and tried to get up but fell back onto the ground, exhausted by fatigue and hunger.

At the price of terrible suffering, the animal had crossed rivers, climbed mountains and traveled over half of Europe to find his friend, who was fortunately able to restore Moffino to life.

In his *Memorial de Sainte-Hélène*, Napoleon tells how moved he was by the sight of a dog on the battlefield who was barking woefully at the side of his master's corpse.

Still more heroic was the exploit of another dog, *White Paw*. He followed a second lieutenant in the French army called Burat, who was the color-bearer in the 116th regiment of the line. One day the soldier's detachment was surrounded by the enemy. The stave of the flag broke but the officer managed to grab the flag. He had already put some of his attackers

Lifting a leg: more than a hygienic operation.

out of action when he received a saber cut on the head. Someone snatched the colors from his hand but he had the strength to get hold of it again. Then, run through with bayonet wounds, Burat fell and was about to be given the coup de grâce when he heard a dog barking. "Help me, White Paw," he cried, and immediately the dog flew at the throat of the enemy soldier who had taken the flag, killing him. Burat seized his standard and a scrap of silk, lost consciousness and fell to the ground at the moment when the harassed enemy withdrew.

White Paw licked his face and revived him. When the Lieutenant opened his eyes, restored to consciousness by the gentle licking, he saw that the poor animal's intestines were spewing out of a large wound; he dragged himself to a nearby stream, ripped off his tie, and soaked it in the water.

Having dressed his companion's wound, he fell to the ground again. Fortunately, neither man nor animal had been mortally wounded.

Bob was an English dog who loved an English soldier with all his heart. During the Crimean campaign, Bob followed his master and Queen Victoria's rifle guards; he took part in all the battles around Sebastopol.

Well, well! Good-day
to you.

When evening came he used to sit in the camp beside his wounded friends, looking at them affectionately, as if to console them and show how sorry for them he felt. He licked their hands and by his devotion managed in some way to alleviate their sufferings.

He was so courageous and so devoted that he was awarded a medal and his name was inscribed in the regimental book. When peace was signed and the troops embarked for home, Bob was nowhere to be found. The officers went looking for and discovered him... in the wrong boat. He was brought back home in triumph and in London, on the day when the troops were reviewed by Queen Victoria, Bob had the honor of marching at the head of his company.

Most armies have taken dogs along with them. *Denmark* was a German dog and the first to enter the entrenchments at Düppel; this animal was renowned for his devotion to the wounded. As soon as one of "his" soldiers fell, he went to him, stanched the flow of blood with his tongue and called for help, never leaving his friend until the stretcher-bearers arrived.

During the 1830 Revolution, the insurgent Parisians were attacking the Louvre when a worker fell dead, hit by a bullet; although his dog, who had accompanied

him, was also wounded he remained near his master's body until it was buried. Several days later, a large hearse carried the many victims of the three days' siege to the cemetery. The dog followed the hearse and after the crowd had left, remained at the mass grave, never ceasing his whining. A short time later, the cemetery-keeper found him lifeless, his grief having killed him.

During the 1914-1918 World War, the dog continued to be the fighting man's companion. How many dogs, rounded up in abandoned villages, followed to the trenches masters to whom they had quickly become attached! At the beginning of the campaign, there were so many dogs following the troops that the military authorities had to take action to limit the numbers allowed into the trenches where they were used as look-outs and go-betweens. Then there were the "gate-crashers" who penetrated to the front line, such is the dog's devotion to the soldiers.

Thirteen thousand dogs were used regularly in the Allied armies during the Great War.

After the warriors, who by their devotion, obedience and love became heroic fighters and helped their masters in battle, we give pride of place to rescue dogs who do not hesitate to risk their lives in order

The attraction (as the anti-pathy) that they feel for each other is always shown demonstratively.

to come to our aid, who risk danger to save men and snatch them back from death.

The valiant *Baby* of Newfoundland whose memory is evergreen in the royal castle of Windsor; the proud *Barry* of the Saint Bernard Hospice, who saved 40 people from imminent death and wore on his collar a medal of honor. Some 100 other celebrated dogs are part of the grand and noble history of the canine race.

The Newfoundland and Saint Bernard dogs are the two breeds whose devotion and spirit of sacrifice seem to be hereditary. Let us briefly recall what they have done and are still doing.

In 1497 John Cabot discovered the island of Newfoundland and took possession of it in the name of England's Henry VII, who had given Cabot and his sons, "permission to sail with six English ships to any country in search of unknown lands."

When the first colonists settled on Newfoundland, they discovered many wild animals there, including bears and wolves, but no dogs.

Where then does the splendid breed of dogs that Newfoundland produces today come from and who has helped more than the "Newfoundlands" to the fame of the island? Whitebourne maintains that this

"There is no one who has not noticed the way in which dogs approach each other..." (Alexandre Dumas).

race is descended from a mastiff and a native wolf. This is an unlikely supposition; it is rather difficult to believe that such ferocious parents could give birth to the gentlest, the best of dogs, the most tender of the species' giants.

The Newfoundland dog is tall and sinewy and of graceful build; it is very sturdy and yet at the same time very light. The head is not large but the brain is well developed. There is intelligence and gentleness in the eyes. The fur is generally fine, bushy and soft. The tail is held straight; the one point of resemblance to the wolf, the Newfoundland dog's sworn enemy.

Newfoundland dogs go into the water more willingly than other dogs; they have an obvious predisposition for it, their large paws like a duck's feet, making it easy for them to swim.

To adapt the popular expression, happy as a fish in water, we could say that no one is happier than a Newfoundland dog in water. It seems to be his principal element on which he buoys himself up while playing. This is a dog which loves water as a hunting dog loves the hunt.

Nevertheless, their passion for water is not at all hereditary. Just as it is impossible to stop an otter from jumping into the first river it sees or to keep a young

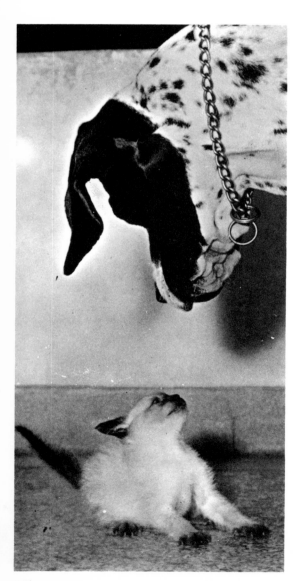

duck hatched by a hen at the edge of a pond, so it is certain that Newfoundland dogs sometimes need to be taught to enjoy the water.

There is a story of several of these dogs which had to be taken by the neck to conquer their aversion for water; but usually their education lasts only one session and as soon as they have touched the water, they break loose and race into it. It has often been noticed that when they are on these occasions scolded, they show how difficult it is for them to obey; in all other circumstances, they seem to try to divine their master's wishes, in order to anticipate them.

But the Newfoundland dog is different from other dogs; not only does he love his master, but at all times he demonstrates his affection and devotion for the whole human race. The list of martyrs is long and in Europe and elsewhere, a record of the names of more than one Newfoundland dog who perished trying to bring help to the shipwrecked has been preserved.

Each country has its own stories to tell. In Holland, a reliable historian related that a traveler was walking on the edge of a canal when suddenly his foot slipped and he fell into the water. A Newfoundland dog saw the unfortunate man floun-

dering in the water and raced to his aid but the man had already lost consciousness and his weight was too much for the animal.

At first, the dog had grabbed the drowning man by the arm but then he realized that the man's head was in the water. Then many spectators, who were watching from the bank, saw the dog stop for a moment, open his mouth and grab the man by the back of the neck in such a way that his face was out of the water.

He soon gave another proof of powers of reflection and intelligence. The banks of the canal were too high and the slope too steep for him to climb with his burden, so he swam well over 500 yards to a spot where he could set the man down. When the people got to the place, he had laid the man on his back and was licking his face to revive him.

The most extraordinary exploits carried

Contrary to an over-simplified opinion, dogs and cats, especially when young, like to play with each other.

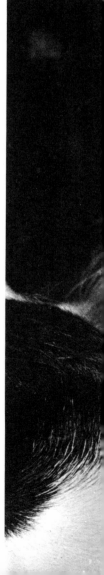

out by dogs deserve to be remembered. The *Durham,* a Sunderland steamer, was shipwrecked near Clay on the coast of Norfolk. The only way in which the crew and passengers could be saved was by making fast on land a ship to shore life-line, but the shore was too far away for a rope to be thrown and the storm was so violent that it was impossible to think of using the lifeboats or swimming to shore.

But on board the ship there was a New-foundland dog; one end of the rescue rope was put into his mouth, and with shining eyes, proud to have understood the impor-tance and difficulty of his task, he jumped into the angry seas; the waves breaking one against the other tossed the poor creature about like a cork as, teeth clench-ed, he fought desperately against them. When, redoubling his efforts, he was near-ing the shore, it was clear that his strength was almost gone. It was then that two sailors, who had been watching this stirring struggle from the shore, jumped into the water and managed to seize and help the dog; thanks to the selfless devotion of all three, the crew was saved.

Some unusual adventure story could be told about nearly every Newfoundland dog. A young English officer, who was an excellent swimmer, had taught one of these dogs to play at leap-frog in the water. To the great amusement of spec-tators, master and dog plunged into the water by turns.

One day, the officer dived and did not reappear. The worried dog looked to right and to left; all at once he understood that something extraordinary had happen-ed: he too dived and was lucky enough to bring the unconscious young man to the surface. Otherwise, the officer cer-tainly would have drowned. Who would dare, after that, to deny that these animals have intelligence and initiative!

During the terrible storms which raged throughout the winter of 1789, an English ship which had sailed from Newcastle, was shipwrecked near Yarmouth. Every-thing was swallowed up by the waves. Not without difficulty, the only survivor, a Newfoundland dog, managed to get to the shore, carrying the captain's wallet in his mouth. The spectators, who had hastily gathered on the shore, tried to pry the wallet free; but in vain for he knew its value, thanks undoubtedly to his master's parting injunction. After having looked at the men for some time, he went up to a venerable looking old man and, without hesitating, gave him the wallet. Then back he went into the sea and until nightfall brought back to land all the

wreckage from the ship that he could carry. This narrative is in a serious English work on natural history.

The Great Saint Bernard in the Alps, was at one time called Mont Jupiter and was later corrupted to Mont Joux. Formerly, a temple dedicated to Jupiter, stood there and traces of it can still be seen. During the excavation work, sacrificial utensils, medals and statues, both large and small, were found.

At this altitude, winter lasts for eight or nine months, the temperature often falling to —27°; even in the middle of summer, it freezes every night. No more than ten days of the year go by without storms, whirlwinds or thick fog.

The ice, pulverized to dust, and the snow are driven before the wind, and snowbanks 20 to 30 feet high build up which can cause avalanches, burying the paths. Victims of cold or hunger, countless travelers have died trying to cross the St. Bernard pass.

On the Great Saint Bernard there is a famous Hospice inhabited by monks whose mission it is to aid people who have been taken unawares by avalanches.

The St. Bernard, the dog who accompanies the monks when they go in search of the unfortunate victims, has great sagacity and a marvelous instinct. Not

Princess Anne, *a six month old Corgi, and her great friend, 60 day old* Angels: *happy puppyhood. Below:* Molly: *a most unexpected role.*

only can he get the scent of human beings while still a long way off, but he is able to take hold of them by their clothing without hurting them at all, then to drag them towards the Hospice, help them to walk and indicate to them that around his neck are hung small bottles of brandy to revive them.

It is only at the cost of terrible exhaustion that these courageous Saint Bernards manage to carry out these rescues; sometimes their legs stiffen up as a result of the cold and have to be rubbed with alcohol to get the circulation going again. Almost all of them end up crippled with pain and, with rare exceptions, Saint Bernards do not live much more than eight years. Quite often they do not even live to that age because they are not, anymore than are the travelers, spared by the avalanches. One year all the dogs died. The monks of the Hospice were obliged to ask for the return of two dogs whom they had given away and so they were able to perpetuate the species. The most famous of the Saint Bernards were Jupiter, Flag and Barry.

In his book on the Alps Tschudi wrote that Barry's zeal was truly extraordinary. If some storm or snow-laden storm cloud was approaching from afar, the dog was restless and nothing could keep him in the monastery. Barking, he sought out the most dreaded spots and searched them unceasingly. One day in a grotto of ice he found a lost child, half-frozen and numbed by that sleep which leads to death. He began to lick him, to warm him until he succeeded in waking him; then by his gestures he managed to make the child understand that he should get on his back and put his arms around his neck. Barry returned in triumph to the Hospice with his precious burden. This dog, who was at the Hospice in 1800 when the French army crossed the pass, had the unusual habit of obliging all the individual soldiers he met to present arms; he barred the passage until they had obeyed.

At least 40 lost travelers were rescued by Barry, more than were saved by any of the other famous St. Bernards. He was unusually lucky in finding them; then he would gently guide those who could still walk and somehow or other he managed to drag or carry the others. He was a hero among heroes.

One stormy night, a traveler saw a huge beast, mouth agape, advancing towards him through the swirling mists. Thinking himself to be in danger, the traveler raised his metal stick and struck out with all his might. The animal fell at his feet, moaning in agony. It was Barry. The monks

Below: Lolita. *This three month old cheetah also has confidence in dogs...*

found him and lavished every care on him, doing everything for him that would have been done for a human being. He was taken to the hospital in Berne but all in vain for his brain had been damaged and he died after long suffering. He was honored in the only possible way. His body was preserved and it now occupies a special place in the city of Berne's museum.

Dogs have an abiding love of children and are their devoted protectors.

A disagreeable countrywoman, nick-named Stony because of her hard heart, married a widower with several children, one of whom, Benoît, was deaf and dumb. The stepmother detested the boy and showered abuse on him. Stony's father came to see her and gave her an Alsatian puppy. The miserly woman was not at all pleased to receive a present of this kind for not only would the dog bring her no profit but it cost her several pieces of bread a day. But if she frightened her husband, she in turn was terrified of her father and so she promised to keep the dog.

Little by little, the puppy grew to be an agile and strong dog. The ground resounded like a drum under his muscular paws and impetuous leaping. Hence the name of Drum, laughingly given him by

Unexpected friendships...

The romance of the pointer Amber with a four month old llama.

one of the village boys, stuck to him from then on.

As the dog grew, his native intelligence made him sense that he was in a bad house; he began to hate Stony and to become attached to the little Benoît. While Drum was weak and learning to walk, it was to Benoît that he went looking for consolation and refuge when the mistress of the house beat or threatened him. Later the roles were reversed: instead of the dog being sustained by Benoît, it was he who courageously stood up for and defended the boy.

Whenever Stony, her face like thunder, advanced upon the child Drum stood facing her and stopped her with his fierce look and low growling.

Once she wanted to defy him; all of a sudden he rose to his full height and putting his two big paws on her chest, showed her a double row of fearsome teeth which scared her so much that she almost fell over backwards. After that, Stony was frightened whenever she heard Drum bark and she took good care of Benoît.

What mother does not trust implicitly the dog of the house? Not without reason, she might hesitate to leave her

children in the care of a maid, but she willingly leaves them, to be watched over by one of those good Pyrenean dogs who are gentler than lambs when playing with the children left in their care, but fierce as lions to strangers and those who would harm their charges.

From time immemorial, dog and child have understood each other very well. At the turn of the century, while the ruins of Pompeii were being excavated, the skeleton of a dog was discovered next to that of a ten or twelve year old child and soon after a collar with curious engravings was also uncovered. On it there was a Greek inscription saying that the dog's name was Delta and that he had belonged to Severinus whose life he had saved three times. The first time he rescued him from drowning, then he chased away four robbers who had attacked his master, and the third time he had wrenched his master from the savage clutches of a she-wolf whose cubs Severinus had tried to steal while in a wood situated near Herculaneum and dedicated to Diana. Finally, concluded the inscription, Delta had attached himself to one of the children of the house and accepted food only from his hand.

If, in spite of all these brave deeds, there are still those who do not hesitate to mistreat dogs, let us just mention the case of the Englishman who, seeing his dog jump into the ocean, jumped after him in order to compel the captain to stop the ship.

The newspapers recently carried the story of a man who was drowned trying to save his dog. It is good to know that we, sometimes, return the dog's devotion.

It is the dog's devotion that offers a ray of light in the following story, which is a shining example of the dog's goodness. A young man, who wanted to drown his dog, took him in a boat far from the shore and on reaching midstream seized the animal and threw him into the river. The instinct of self-preservation is no less strong in dogs than in man and so the dog, who had at first disappeared under the water, came up to the surface and made desperate efforts to get back to the boat, but each time he was about to reach it his master pushed him away with an oar.

This barbarous struggle between man and dog lasted quite a while, then the man lost patience and, catching hold of the oar with both hands, struck the dog a heavy

blow on the head. However, in doing so, the man lost his balance and fell into the water.   At that moment, the scene changed from the cruel to the sublime, for the dog dived after his master, seized him and brought him back to shore, after having, over and over again, narrowly missed being carried away by the current.

Curious familiarity

Portrait of the Dog

Stature, elegance of form, strength of body, freedom of movement, none of these outer qualities represents what is most noble in a living being: since we prefer a man's wit to his figure, courage to strength, feeling to beauty, we believe that the inner qualities are the most noble in the animal too. Because of them he differs from the automaton and comes close to us. It is feeling that ennobles, governs and quickens his being, commands the organs, makes the limbs active, awakens desire and gives forward movement, will and life to matter.

The animal's perfection therefore depends on perfection of feeling; the broader the range of his feeling, the greater his faculties and resources, the more intense his existence and his relations with the rest of the universe. And when the feeling is sensitive and can be perfected through training, the animal becomes worthy of entering into the society of man. The dog knows how to cooperate with man in his plans, watch over his safety, help and defend him, please him, how to gain his master's good will and captivate him by his devoted services and repeated endearments, thus transforming a tyrant into a protector.

The dog, independent of the beauty of his form, his liveliness, his strength and his agility, has par excellence all the inner qualities that can attract man's attention. The wild dog is dangerous to all animals because of his fiery, ferocious and blood-thirsty nature. But in the domestic dog this gives way to the gentlest feelings and the pleasure of attaching himself to man, the desire to please and to lay his courage, strength and talents at his master's feet. He awaits his master's orders for the joy of carrying them out, he consults, questions, begs; one glance is sufficient to make him understand his master's will. Without the capacity of thought that man has, the dog has all the warmth of feeling; and, even more than man, the dog has fidelity and constancy in his affections: he has no ambition, no self-interest, no desire for vengeance, no fear other than that of displeasing; he is all zeal, ardor, obedience. More sensitive to memories of kindness than of injury, he is not discouraged by mistreatment but submits to it, forgetting or remembering it only in order to become more attached. Far from being annoyed or running away, the dog lets himself in for new trials and meets them with only a whine, licking the hand that has just beat him. In the long run he placates the hand through patience and submission.

More docile than man, more tractable

than any other animal, not only does the dog learn quickly but he even conforms to the gestures, the manners and all the habits of those who give him orders. He takes on the tone of the house where he lives; like the other servants, he is disdainful in the homes of the great and boorish in the country. Always zealous for his master's interests and attentive to his friends, the dog pays no attention to people who show no interest in him and is against those who seem to be there just to bother him; he recognizes them by their voices, clothes and gestures and makes them keep their distance. When he has been told to guard the house at night, he becomes prouder and sometimes fierce; he stays up, makes the rounds, is aware of strangers who are still a long way off, and should they stop or try to enter the premises, he rushes at them and, while fighting them, sounds the alarm by persistent and angry barking. He is as furious against predatory human beings as against carnivorous animals; he leaps at them, biting and tearing at them until he manages to snatch away what they are trying to steal. Then, pleased with his victory, he settles down beside the spoils, not even touching them to satisfy his hunger. By his actions he shows his capacity for courage, moderation, loyalty.

Games and high spirits.

After having enjoyed it, the dog is extremely attracted to the water.

Always courageous, in the trough of a giant wave.

To imagine for a moment that the canine species had never existed is to make ourselves aware of its importance in nature's order. Without the dog's help, how could man conquer, train and make slaves of the other animals? How could he, even today, discover, hunt and destroy wild and harmful animals? To make himself safe and to become master of the living universe, man had to start by selecting likely types of animals. Then, in order to be able to use them against the other beasts, he had to win over with kindness and gentleness those who were capable of becoming attached to and obeying humans. Thus man's first accomplishment was the education of the dog, and the fruit of that achievement was the conquest and peaceful possession of the earth.

Most animals are swifter, more agile, stronger and even more courageous than man: nature has equipped and armed them better. Moreover, their senses, especially their sense of smell, are much more highly developed. To have won over to our side as brave and docile a species as the dog is to have acquired new senses and powers which we otherwise lack. The machines and instruments that we have invented to perfect our other senses and to increase their range do not, even in their usefulness, come near to those ready-made ones that nature offers us. Making up for the imperfection of our sense of smell, they have placed in our hands powerful and permanent means of conquering and ruling. The dog, faithful to man, will always maintain a measure of power, a degree of superiority over the other animals; he commands them, he rules over a flock where his voice carries more authority than the shepherd's: safety, order and discipline are the fruits of his vigilance and his activity; he reigns over subjects whom he leads and protects, and against whom he never uses force except to keep the peace. But it is mainly in a fight against enemy or self-reliant animals that his courage has full play and his intelligence is used to its maximum: here natural talents unite with acquired qualities. As soon as the noise of battle is heard, as soon as the sound of the hunter's horn or his voice has given the signal of impending battle, eyes aglow with fresh ardor, the dog is almost beside himself with joy: by his actions and his yelping, he signals his impatience to fight and his desire to win: then, as he walks in silence, he reconnoitres the country, to discover and to surprise the enemy in his stronghold. He tries to find his tracks and follows them step by step. Then by the different intonations in his barking he

"The dog hunts with method and always with success."

The pleasure of retrieving things, particular to the hunting dog, is evident in the most varied circumstances.

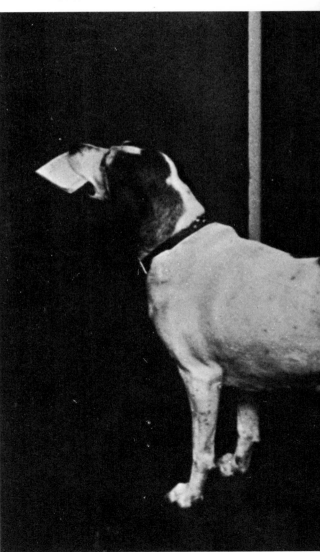

indicates time and distance, the species and even the age of the animal he is tracking.

The fondness for hunting or war is common to animals and ourselves: uncicilized man only knows how to fight and hunt. All carnivorous animals, who like flesh and have the means and the strength, are natural hunters. The lion and the tiger, whose strength is so great that they are sure to win, hunt alone without art; wolves, foxes, wild dogs, join together, understand and help each other, take turns or share the prey; and when training has perfected this natural talent in the domestic dog, when he has been taught to curb his ardor, moderate his movements, and has gotten used to a regular pace and a form of discipline, indispensable to the art of hunting, he hunts with method and always with success.

It can be said that the dog is the only animal whose fidelity is put to the test; the only one who always knows his master and the friends of the house, the only one who senses when a stranger arrives; who hears his name and recognizes the voices of "his" family. Again, he is the only one who does not rely solely on himself, the only one who, when lost, helps his master to find him, by whimpering and whining. The dog alone can find his way again after having made a long

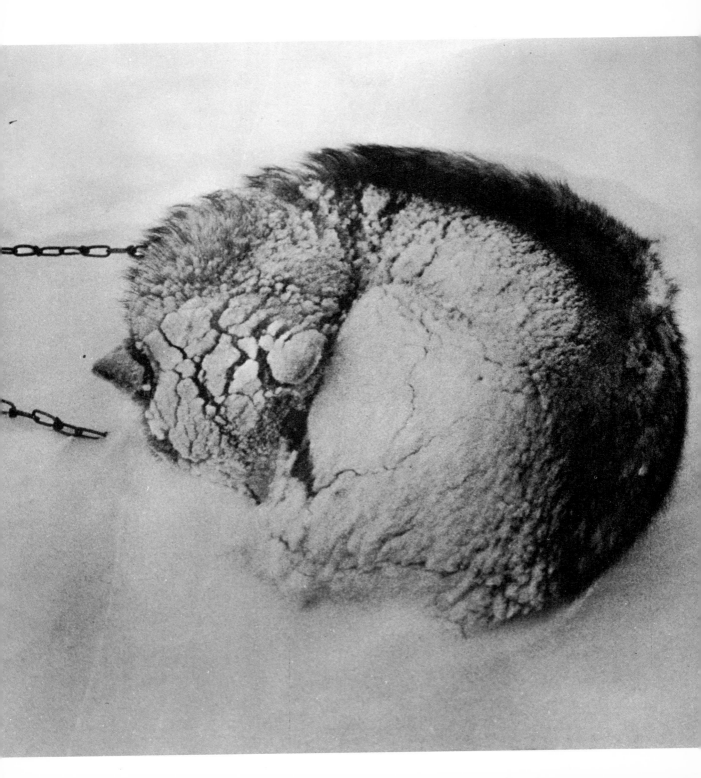

journey only once and finally, the dog is the only one whose natural talents are evident and whose education is always successful.

Of all the animals, the dog is the one whose nature is the most impressionable, most easily influenced by change, according to the mood of the moment or how he is being treated. He is also the one whose nature is most subject to the variations and alterations caused by physical influences: temperament, abilities, bodily habits vary enormously. Even the form is not constant; in the same country one dog is very different from another and the species is, so to speak, very different from itself in different climates. From this there results that confusion, that mixture and such an enormous variety of races that they cannot be counted: hence such marked differences in height, build, bodily appearance, length of the muzzle, shape of the head, length and direction of the ears and the tail, the color, quality and quantity of fur, etc.; so that there is nothing that is constant, nothing common to these animals except the similarity of their internal organism and their ability to reproduce together; and as those who differ most from each other in all respects nevertheless reproduce individuals who can perpetuate themselves by reproducing other individuals, it is clear that all dogs, however different or varied, are only one and the same species.

But the difficult thing to grasp in this great variety of different races, is the character of the primitive race, the original race, the race which is mother of all the others: how does one determine the effects of climate, food, etc.? How are they to be distinguished from the other effects or rather the results which come from the mixture of these different races among themselves, either as wild or domestic animals? The fact is that, with time, all these causes change the most constant form and nature's imprint does not retain all its pureness in the objects that man has handled a great deal. Those animals who are independent enough to make their own choice of climate and food are the most successful in retaining this original imprint; and it can be accepted that, among such animals, the first and oldest of the species is still pretty faithfully represented today by its descendents: but the form of those which man has subjugated and has transported from one climate to another, whose food, habits and way of life he has changed, must have changed more than all the others; and indeed in domestic animals there is much more variety of species than among wild animals: and since, the dog is the most closely attached to man of all domestic

The training and the social role of the German shepherd.

The dog has always warned man of danger. Does the role performed by the one we see here surprise us? His task carried out, he falls asleep with a clear conscience.

animals, the one who, living like man, also has the most irregular life; the one in whom feeling is sufficiently in control to make him docile, obedient and susceptible to any impression and even any restraint, it is not surprising that he, of all the animals, is also the one in whom there are the greatest varieties of form, build, color and all other qualities.

Several other circumstances contribute to this alteration. The dog has a short life; he reproduces often and in comparatively large numbers; and since he is constantly before man's eyes, as soon as, by an accident of nature, singularities or apparent variations have been found in some dogs, man has sought to perpetuate them by crossing these odd strains—as is still done today when new races of dogs or other animals are desired. Besides, although all the species are equally old— the number of generations since creation being much greater in the species whose members live only a short time—the variations, the alterations, even the degree of degeneration, must have become more considerable, just because these animals are farther away from their origin than those who live linger. Man is today eight times closer to Adam than the dog is to the first dog since man lives eighty years and the dog only ten. If then, for whatever cause it might be, these two species tended to degenerate in equal measure, the alteration would today be eight times more pronounced in the dog than in man.

Photos : Atlas 59 b, 80 d, 131 b - Ballard/Atlas 59 a - Barey/Atlas 35 - Bartl/Bavaria 19 a, b - Bas/Bavaria 32 a - Baumann/Bavaria 60 b - Beringer & Pampaluchi 2, 49, 58, 81 d, 89, 100, 118, 121, 123 b, 125, end papers - Betzler/Bavaria 64 a, 75 a, b - Binanzer/Bavaria 80 e - Bodmer/Bavaria 82 - Bocher/Atlas 54 a - Bramoss/Bavaria 70 - Bresson/Atlas 8 b - Buthaud/Jacana 136 a, b - Camera Press/Sirman 81 a, 104 a, b, 142 - Cevaër/Atlas 55 a - Ceyrac/Atlas 23 b - Chapman/Fotogram 12 b, 40 b - Chavaud de Rochefort/Fotogram 8 a - Chevalier/Jacana 127 - Cleare/Sirman 135 - Comet 24, 36, 52 a, b, 55 b, 105, 107 a, 122, 131 a, 132 - Davey/Camera Press/Sirman 4 - Dapra/Bavaria 44, 85 a - Debru/Fotogram 17 - Doidge/Camera/Sirman 45 a - Dourian/Fotogram 64 c - Drysdale/Camera/Sirman 11, 23 a, 33, 78, 108 b, 112 a, 114 a, b, 115 a, b, 129 c - Dubois/Jacana 73 - Dupille/Jacana 34 b - Escudero/Fotogram 99, 109 - Esten/Camera/Sirman 79 a - Fenzl/Bavaria 61 b - Feeré/Fotogram 46 c, 47 a, 50, 80 c, 88, 90 a - Fischer/Bavaria 129 a - Fleury/Fotogram 47 b, 81 e, 90 b - Fox/Atlas 20 b - Frass/Atlas 25, 81 b - Frese/Bavaria 75 - Frieman/Fotogram 6 a, b, c, d, 27, 94 a, - Gabanou/Fotogram 80, 87 b - Gajda/Camera/Sirman 96 a, b, 97, 108 a - Gescheidt/Camera/Sirman 43 - Globe/Sirman 110, 141 - Gooth/Bavaria 68 - Gundel/Bavaria 46 b - Hamilton/Camera/Sirman 29, 62 b - Hamilton/Globe/Sirman 112 b, 113 - Harrington/Camera/Sirman 133 - Henrion/Jacana 59 c - Henty/Camera/Sirman 103 a, b, 116, 117 - Hewet/Globe/Sirman 30 b, 124, 138 a, b, c, 139 - Heyn/Camera/Sirman 107 b - Interfoto/Bavaria 51 b - Isselin/Fotogram 93 - Jarret/Jacana 64 b, 91 - Jöst/Bavaria 129 b - Jouanne/Atlas 54 b - König/Bavaria 56 - Loncel/Fotogram 26 - Lovat/Atlas 85 b - Martin/Fotogram 28 - Martinerie/Fotogram 57, 98 - M. de Massas/Fotogram 15 - Meerkämper/Bavaria 60 a - Merlet/Atlas 46 a - Mitchell/Camera/Sirman 38, 39 - Moore/Atlas 9, 34 a - Müller/Bavaria 31 a, 45 b - Niestlé/Bavaria 41 - Orr/Camera/Sirman 77 b - Parente/Fotogram 12 a, 31 b, 63 - Pedone/Bavaria 18 - Peerless/Camera/Sirman 77 a - Pictorial Press/Sirman 140 - Pivecks/Bavaria 123 a, 143 - Poinsot/Jacana 72, 74 - Popper/Atlas 61 a, 86 a, b, c, 130 - Prenzel/Sirman 17 - Rademacher/Camera/Sirman 101 - Reporters Ass./Sirman 95 - Rittings/Comet 20 a - Saint-Clar/Atlas 64 d, 71, 83 - Schindelbeck/Bavaria 71 - Schelgel/Bavaria 48 - Schmachtenberger/Bavaria 76 - Scheiders/Bavaria 22, 84 b, 144 - Severin/Sirman 111 - Sirman 94 - Staincq/Atlas 120 - Szymonski (von)/Bavaria 84 a - Tercafs/Jacana 80 a - Thoby/Ifot 51 a - Varga/Fotogram 32 b - Verson/Fotogram 87 a - Viollet 30 a, 66 a, b - Visage/Jacana 128 - Wagner/Bavaria 40 a - Wehmeyer/Bavaria 69 - Wing/Camera/Sirman 107 c - Wippet 62 a - Withers/Atlas 61 c - Zeitbild/Bavaria 79 b.

Printed in Italy by Istituto Italiano d'Arti Grafiche, Bergamo